The Spontaneity Shop in
with King's Head Theatre presents

BREXIT

This production officially opened at
the King's Head Theatre on
Thursday 13 June 2019

Brexit was first performed at The Pleasance Courtyard as part of the Edinburgh Fringe, 1-25 August 2018, with the following cast:

Cast

ADAM MASTERS	Timothy Bentinck
PAUL CONNELL	Mike McShane
DIANA PURDY	Pippa Evans
HELENA BRANDT	Jo Caulfield
SIMON CAVENDISH	Hal Cruttenden

Brexit premiered at the King's Head Theatre, London on 30 October 2018 with the following cast and production team:

Cast

ADAM MASTERS	Timothy Bentinck
PAUL CONNELL	Adam Astill
DIANA PURDY	Pippa Evans
HELENA BRANDT	Lucy Montgomery
SIMON CAVENDISH	Thom Tuck

Production Team

Writer	Robert Khan
Writer/Director	Tom Salinsky
Lighting Director	Nicholas Holdridge
Music & Sound Designer	Jamie Robertson
Assistant Director	Charlie Norburn
Producer	Jason Smith
Graphic Designer	Jonathan Monkhouse

Brexit opened at the King's Head Theatre, London on 11 June 2019 with the following cast and production team:

Cast

ADAM MASTERS	David Benson
PAUL CONNELL	Adam Astill
DIANA PURDY	Jessica Fostekew
HELENA BRANDT	Margaret Cabourn-Smith
SIMON CAVENDISH	Thom Tuck

Production Team

Writer	Robert Khan
Writer / Director	Tom Salinsky
Lighting Director	Nicholas Holdridge
Music & Sound Designer	Jamie Robertson
Assistant Director	Alex Hick
Stage Manager	Ally Southern
Producer	Jason Smith
Graphic Designer	Jonathan Monkhouse

King's Head Theatre Timeline

The King's Head Theatre is 48 years old, here are just a few of the highlights of our journey so far...

1970   Dan Crawford founds the first pub theatre in London since Shakespeare's day and the King's Head Theatre is born.

1983   A revival of *Mr Cinders*, starring Joanna Lumley, opens at the King's Head Theatre before transferring to the West End. It goes on to run for 527 performances.

1986   Maureen Lipman stars in the Olivier Award nominated *Wonderful Town* at the King's Head Theatre.

1988   Premier of Tom Stoppard's *Artist Descending a Staircase* opens at the King's Head Theatre before transferring to Broadway.

1991   Steven Berkoff directs and stars in the UK premiere of *Kvetch* at the King's Head Theatre.

1992   Trainee Resident Directors Scheme wins Royal Anniversary Trust Award.

2010   Opera Up Close, founded by Adam Spreadbury-Maher and Robin Norton-Hale become resident company for 4 years.

2011   *La bohème* wins the Olivier Award for Best New Opera Performance.

2015   King's Head Theatre forms a new charity to secure the future of the theatre. *Trainspotting* is first performed at the King's Head Theatre – in August 2017 it hit it's 900th performance.

2016   43,857 audience members see a show at our London home - our highest footfall ever.

2017   King's Head Theatre announces the transfer of *La bohème* & *Strangers in Between* to Trafalgar Studios 2 in London's West End. *La bohème* goes on to be nominated for Best New Opera Production at the Olivier Awards.

2019   King's Head Theatre's production of Kevin Elyot's *Coming Clean* transfers to Trafalgar Studios 2 in London's West End.

2020   King's Head Theatre moves to its new permanent home in Islington Square, securing the future of the venue for generations to come.

Robert Khan and Tom Salinsky

BREXIT

OBERON BOOKS
LONDON

WWW.OBERONBOOKS.COM

First published in 2018 by Oberon Books Ltd
521 Caledonian Road, London N7 9RH
Tel: +44 (0) 20 7607 3637 / Fax: +44 (0) 20 7607 3629
e-mail: info@oberonbooks.com
www.oberonbooks.com

PB ISBN: 9781786826787
E ISBN: 9781786826770

Cover design: Jonathan Monkhouse

eBook conversion by Lapiz Digital Services, India.

10 9 8 7 6 5 4 3 2

Characters

Rt Hon Adam Masters MP
Prime Minister

Paul Connell
Senior Political Consultant

Rt Hon Diana Purdy MP
Secretary of State for Exiting the European Union

Rt Hon Simon Cavendish DL MP
Secretary of State for International Trade

Helena Brandt
Chief EU Negotiator

Lights snap on. Noise. Hubbub.

The House of Commons. RT HON ADAM MASTERS MP, the Prime Minister, full of confidence on his first day, stands behind a desk with a dispatch box on it with a stand microphone. ADAM is finishing his previous answer as MPs cheer and boo...

ADAM: I can assure him – I can assure him of that!

ADAM sits down again.

SPEAKER: *Order, order. Next question please for the Prime Minister, Mr Adam Masters. David Pilgrim.*

PILGRIM: *Thank you Mr Speaker. I welcome our new Prime Minister to his post! Can he recall a post-war leader with as much potential, as much sheer charisma...*

HON. MEMS: *Ask a proper question! Give him a job! Who is this toady? [etc. etc.]*

SPEAKER: *That's enough flattery. The Prime Minister...*

ADAM rises to give his answer.

ADAM: My thanks to my Right Honourable Friend, for his welcome. I'm sure this will be the first of many such ruthless interrogations.

BARRON: *Resign!*

ADAM: All things come to those who wait.

Hon. Mems laughter.

SPEAKER: *Order! Sam Barron.*

BARRON: *Leading a Tory government that has no majority, is divided between its right wing, its left wing and all the other wings in between, does the Prime Minister agree that his first act should be the calling of a general election?*

Hon. Mems. simultaneously cheer and boo.

ADAM: *[Rises.]* I will take no lessons in unity from her Labour party, his Labour party or indeed any of the other five Labour parties now represented in this House!

Hon. Mems. cheer.

SPEAKER: *Patrick Brostoff.*

BROSTOFF: *On a matter of high constitutional import…*

HON. MEMS: *Oh no! Not him again!*

BROSTOFF: *Will the Prime Minister confirm his Government's desire to serve all parts of these islands with rigour, duty and without any special favours?*

HON. MEMS: *Unless they're Irish! Send them another bung!*

ADAM: I can promise my Honourable Friend that he will shortly see a more United Kingdom than he has ever seen before!

Hon. Mems cheer and boo.

Lights fade…

SCENE TWO

The Prime Minister's office in the House of Commons. PAUL CONNELL (morose, world-weary, Canadian) is perched on a desk which has a green lamp, behind which is a captain's chair. ADAM is thumbing through some papers.

ADAM enters, beaming with delight.

ADAM: He shoots! He scores!

ADAM runs around the office, fists clenched in delight. Eventually he notices PAUL looking at him impassively.

ADAM: Come on Paul. That was good. I never realised PMQs could be so much fun. Why did my predecessors make such hard work of it? The Used Car Salesman always sounded like he was cheerfully announcing redundancies on the factory floor – and as for Matron, Christ almighty.

PAUL: I'm glad you had fun, Adam.

ADAM: Have you seen the polls? My ratings are higher than those reserved for third world dictators. I could give the Khmer Rouge a run for its money. Even you must be pleased.

PAUL: It's meaningless. It's a political honeymoon. The bastards are still too busy fighting among themselves to really hold you to account.

ADAM: I suppose every new PM gets a bit of leeway from the Opposition.

PAUL: I'm talking about your backbenchers.

ADAM: Why can't you just be happy for me?

PAUL: Andrew Bonar Law.

ADAM: What?!

PAUL: Bonar Law served for two hundred and eleven days. You have two hundred and five further days to go before you outlast the unknown prime minister.

ADAM: Remind me never to ask you to do my best man's speech.

PAUL: I did do your best man's speech.

ADAM: I remember… listen, I know I said I wouldn't need you after the campaign was over, but it turns out I could really use a chief of staff. When Matron went, she took everyone with her, so Number Ten is drastically under-powered. I've currently got a tea-lady running pensions policy and my chauffeur is having to bone up on who's in and who's out in the Kremlin.

PAUL: I'm a campaign manager. And your campaign was successfully managed, so I'm going back to my consultancy. I'm sure you can find yourself a chief of staff who will celebrate your empty victories with the enthusiasm you're looking for.

ADAM: Come on, Paul. What will it take? We can get pissed together and trash Chequers. You can take HMS Ark Royal for a spin around Southampton harbour. We can even play with the big you-know-what button. If only I could remember the password. Actually, I should really write that down somewhere for security.

PAUL holds out a file.

PAUL: Any help I could offer, I've put down in here.

ADAM takes the file. He opens it and looks through.

ADAM: Oh, this is brilliant. Ah… now that's a masterstroke… you're a real political Svengali.

PAUL: You're not reading it, are you?

ADAM: Why don't you summarise?

PAUL: Okay. Point one. Watch out for ticking time bombs.

ADAM: Time bombs?

PAUL: Your so-called majority is still only propped up by a handful of Looney Tunes from across the Irish Sea. Then you've got Brexiteers carrying out death rituals in Central Office over the latest proposals from Brussels, while Remainers continue to maraud the Commons like a touring version of Lord of The Flies. I've also heard your new Education Secretary is going on Desert Island Discs this Sunday with a play list including "The Times They are A-Changing", "I'm Still Standing" and "Don't Stop Me Now".

ADAM: I can deal with Derek Gadd. Anything else?

PAUL: Point two. You need a full cabinet.

ADAM: *[Indignant.]* Well, I <u>do</u> have a full cabinet… very, very nearly.

PAUL: You haven't appointed either a Trade or a Brexit Secretary.

ADAM: You have to understand – I'm playing political Jenga. One false move on Europe and the whole Cabinet collapses again.

PAUL: The country needs you to start making progress. The negotiating period was supposed to last eighteen months. That was three years ago.

ADAM: *[Petulant.]* Fine, I'll appoint people. *[Then, more eagerly.]* So you'll stay?

PAUL: Point three. You need a major policy announcement to demonstrate your authority. Take the opportunity to set the agenda.

ADAM: I don't suppose you have any ideas about what my major policy announcement should be do you?

PAUL: Read the file.

ADAM: I think we both know I'm never going to do that.

PAUL: Okay, listen. The purpose of the Brexit department is negotiating the final trade relationship with the EU. Meanwhile an entirely separate Trade department is trying to negotiate trade with the rest of the world. You have two mutually contradictory departments in one government. Show your decisiveness by merging them into one.

ADAM: That's brilliant.

PAUL: All part of your united and principled government.

ADAM: "United and principled government". Yes, I like that.

PAUL: I have my moments. Shall I start drafting the announcement?

ADAM: Oh, well, there's no immediate hurry is there?

PAUL: No… hurry? Sky News is camping on the doorstep, the BBC has three helicopters flying overhead and Channel Four is so hungry for news it's sent its fastest moped. And you only have weeks at most in which you can actually get things done, before "Thank goodness for a change at last!" turns into "Jesus, not this guy again." If you're going to make a success of Brexit, you need to start now. Today!

ADAM: That reminds me… which way did you vote?

PAUL: What difference does that make?

ADAM: I just realised. I've never asked you.

PAUL: Which way did _you_ vote?

ADAM: As is a matter of public record, I voted remain in the referendum – but were the choice to be presented again, I would gladly vote leave.

PAUL: Wow. You've turned political ambiguity into a message from God.

ADAM: It's a gift. So – you'll do it?

PAUL: What's the point? It's not like you'd follow any of my advice.

ADAM: Paul, I trust you completely. Anything you ask of me, I'll do.

PAUL: You've refused to follow my advice three times in the last two minutes!!

ADAM: I have a Brexit strategy. But I need you by my side to deliver it.

PAUL: Then let's start by filling these last two cabinet posts. Who's on the list?

ADAM: Well, when you take out all the people who can't be trusted, can't do the job, are clinically insane, or I've already given them something else to do, there aren't that many names left.

PAUL: But there are some names left?

ADAM: One or two.

PAUL: So, you don't need me to put a "help wanted" sign in the window?

ADAM: I wouldn't rule it out.

PAUL: Why? *[Suddenly suspicious.]* Adam… who do you have left on the list?

ADAM silently hands PAUL a laminated call-list.

PAUL: You've got to be kidding.

Blackout.

SCENE THREE

A corridor in the Commons. SIMON CAVENDISH DL MP (polite, donnish, pin-striped) is tapping at his iPhone. DIANA PURDY MP (direct, passionate, chaotic) marches the other way. She is talking rapidly into her phone.

DIANA: No, no, I never said the Chancellor couldn't count. Yes… the quote about needing an instruction manual for the abacus can stay, but you didn't hear it from me, otherwise tomorrow's obituary column will include your own. Love and hugs!

She hangs up.

DIANA: Journalists… Ah Simon. Why are you lurking here? Surely you can't have a sudden gap in your busy media schedule?

SIMON: Actually, Diana, I was hoping I might have a word with you.

DIANA: Did Loose Women drop you for an item about deoderising lampshades?

SIMON: I know that you understand the vast esteem in which I hold you.

DIANA: Just get on with it, Simon. Surely even you can retire the smug and smarm show for a moment?

SIMON: When you say smarm I say courtesy. Where you detect smugness…

DIANA: Jesus! Are you flirting with me?

SIMON: Certainly not!

DIANA: Well you're behaving very strangely and I don't like it.

SIMON: We live in strange times. Four full days have elapsed since our new Emperor was enthroned and yet still nothing from Number Ten.

DIANA: You thought Adam would give you a job?

SIMON: I had heard some rather… exotic rumours, but alas it seems that role has gone to someone else.

DIANA: You actually thought you could snare the Foreign Office!? You've never even eaten a croissant.

SIMON: Britain needs a true patriot representing its interests abroad.

DIANA: Is that why the Opposition start singing Land of Hope and Glory every time you rise to speak in the House?

SIMON: I was hoping we could team up – since we both seem to have been passed over. You must have been seething that Derek got Education.

DIANA: There are still a few vacancies. Adam hasn't overlooked me.

SIMON: Not even after that nasty question you threw at him at PMQs? Was that a chiding reference to Ozymandias I noticed?

DIANA: No, I don't think so.

SIMON: It's always such a delight to see new courtiers eager to melt the new king's feet in the regal furnace.

DIANA: No, no, no… I was making him look good. If I'd asked him an easy question then he would think… that I was trying to… you know…

SIMON: I'm almost certain he doesn't bear you any ill-will. You did vote for him after all.

DIANA: Well, you, know… it was that or stand against him.

SIMON: I doubt that would have gone well. Think how the wider party would have reacted when they learned of your plans to move Buckingham Palace to Brussels and translate God Save The Queen into Flemish.

DIANA: Rather like your plans to sink a moat around the home counties and flog off the NHS for spare parts?

SIMON: You see. We're very much alike. And if we can't continue our debate from inside Government, then maybe we should focus on what we can both achieve together, from the back-benches?

DIANA: How do I know that you wouldn't betray me, the second you got the call from Number Ten?

SIMON: As distasteful as it sounds, we may just have to trust each other.

DIANA: Aren't you even going to offer me a backstop?

SIMON: *[Stung.]* I don't think there's any call for that kind of language! This is a very fair offer, Diana.

DIANA: Can I think about it?

SIMON's phone starts ringing in his pocket, the ringtone is "I Vow to Thee, My Country". SIMON doesn't seem to notice.

DIANA: Simon!?

He realises and fishes his phone out of his pocket.

SIMON: Oh… ooh! Do excuse me.

He hovers away.

DIANA: Simon! What about our…!? Simon!!

DIANA doesn't know what to do with herself. Then her own phone rings, the ringtone is Hip-Hop.

DIANA: Yes!? Hello! *[She composes herself.]* Oh – hello!

She marches off.

SCENE FOUR

The Offices of the European Commission in Brussels. There is a globe which doubles as a wine holder. HELENA BRANDT is sitting neatly in an arm chair while ADAM paces fretfully. HELENA has just a touch of a German accent.

HELENA: I just don't know what you think we'll be able to achieve. We've had negotiating teams working together for years now.

ADAM: I thought if we met in person...

HELENA: Yes, I thought the same thing when you were first elected. But our meeting in August was cancelled with two days' notice. Then our meeting in September was cancelled with four days' notice. Then our meeting in October was cancelled two days after it was supposed to have taken place. So, you'll forgive me if I don't find this sudden eagerness for face-to-face talks terribly convincing.

ADAM: I've had a tough few weeks. Is it too much to ask for just a little sympathy?

HELENA: Oh, sympathy you can have. On behalf the EU, we're still all very sorry. For us, Brexit is like a close friend confiding they have contracted a terrible disease. You're full of compassion while being secretly relieved that it isn't actually happening to you.

ADAM: Well, I'm surprised there's no booze. Most European negotiations I've been involved with seemed to be completely organised around free-flowing wine and extravagant lunches.

HELENA: I think we can leave the refreshments until there is a diplomatic breakthrough.

ADAM: You don't want to order some up just in case?

HELENA: No.

ADAM: But, you don't know what I'm going to say…

HELENA: Fine. Go ahead. See if you can find something to say which none of your predecessors has managed to come up with. I'm listening.

ADAM: Okay, good. Thank you.

HELENA: Well…?

ADAM: Well… we need a full and final settlement. We need to be imaginative… to come up with an innovative approach for our future relationship…

HELENA: And this is where it starts.

ADAM: Where what starts?!

HELENA: The point in any meeting with the British when they tell us to be more ambitious. To think big. To open our eyes to the new economic and trading opportunities. Without realising that to us the most ambitious option is known as… membership of the European Union.

ADAM: There is no need to be like that.

HELENA: We want influence. We want independence. We want control. Raindrops and roses and whiskers on kittens. Bright copper kettles and warm woollen mittens. Beef dripping and bunting and piccalilli and passports – Christ, the passports! Resplendent in a violence of blue.

ADAM: I think you're exaggerating.

HELENA: According to your tabloids these are all things we've attempted to ban. I don't even know what is piccalilli!

ADAM: Helena, please! I've got to go back with something or my leadership is over.

HELENA: We're somewhat used to dealing with a regular conveyer belt of UK prime ministers these days. British manufacturing at its clockwork finest.

HELENA looks at him with something like pity. She softens, just a little.

HELENA: Maybe you should have just planned on doing a Norway from the beginning?

ADAM: A Norway?

HELENA: Norway's government applied to join the EU, and we were happy to have them. But not wanting to rush, they first joined the European Economic Area, fully intending to proceed to full membership in due course.

ADAM: But then they lost that referendum.

HELENA: So, plans had to change. However, while deciding upon their next course of action, they opted to stay in the European Economic Area, purely as a brief interim measure.

ADAM: Remind me, when was that?

HELENA: Nineteen ninety-four. Still, you can't rush big decisions. Now, was there anything else you wanted to say?

The lights fade…

SCENE FIVE

ADAM is in his Commons office. DIANA is sitting in a chair at stage left. ADAM is pacing, centre-stage. DIANA stares at him with a mixture of shock and horror.

DIANA: Have you suffered a brain injury?

ADAM: It's a serious offer, Diana. I need a new Brexit Secretary.

DIANA: Me? I'm on record as saying that the upcoming drizzle, disaster and economic recession caused by Brexit will make the Weimar Republic look like a model of fiscal rectitude.

ADAM: I just can't think of a better person for the job.

DIANA: It's a Kamikaze department, whose very existence I have publicly opposed. It's literally the only job in government that I wouldn't want.

ADAM: But it's the only job on offer.

The lighting changes revealing SIMON sitting at stage right and plunging DIANA's side of the stage into darkness.

SIMON: Gosh. Goodness.

ADAM: It's a serious offer, Simon. I think you would make a wonderful Trade Secretary, negotiating the final terms of the deal with our European colleagues.

SIMON: Me? I'm on record as denouncing our Trade Ministry as being so disorganised that it's a crime against public administration. That might make it a bit tricky for me to inspire the team.

ADAM: I just can't think of a better person for the job.

SIMON: But the Trade Ministry is the only job in government that I wouldn't want.

ADAM: Simon, for so long, you've been a political outsider. Yes, you've built up your media profile. The television news is never more than ten minutes away from your flamboyant pocket squares, expensive burgundy and hasty opinions. But who wants to be the Keith Floyd of politics? I'm offering you the chance to become an insider. I'm offering you power.

Back to DIANA.

DIANA: I'm sorry, Adam, the answer is definitely no.

ADAM: Diana, for so long, you've been a political outsider. Holding those junior Ministerial posts. Under-Secretary for Badger Culling. Unpaid Minister for Women's Equality. I'm offering you the chance to become an insider. Part of the group that really makes the decisions. I'm offering you power.

DIANA: That is tempting.

ADAM: I'd give you total autonomy. You could shape the department however you wanted.

Back to SIMON.

SIMON: In that case, I would insist that we immediately commit to a withdrawal from the customs union. Only then can we move forward with the foreign trade deals which we need to stand on our own feet as a nation again.

ADAM: That would mean... ending the transitional arrangements early?

SIMON: Precisely.

ADAM: Wouldn't the economic fall-out create huge unrest? As interest rates soar and inflation and unemployment climb, who knows how the public will react. It might threaten the rule of law, the courts, the police. It could be anarchy...

SIMON: A democracy that doesn't listen to its people isn't a democracy.

ADAM: Very well put.

Back to DIANA.

DIANA: As Brexit secretary, my sole aim would be to ensure that we avoid an act of economic suicide by cancelling all these foreign trade deals so we have a fighting chance of staying in the customs union.

ADAM: That would mean… making the transitional arrangements permanent?

DIANA: Exactly.

ADAM: But wouldn't refusing the will of the people lead to the whole notion of democracy in this country being called into question? It might threaten the rule of law, the courts, the police. It could be anarchy…

DIANA: A democracy that can't change its mind isn't a democracy.

ADAM: Very well put.

Back to SIMON.

SIMON: So, what do you say?

ADAM: It'll create a lot of problems within the party. The left-wingers will accuse us of putting party before country. Maybe I made a mistake in offering you the post.

SIMON: Oh no you don't. Now, listen, Adam. We're currently leaving the EU like the friend you met on holiday who's still at the lodge at two in the morning when everyone else has gone to bed. We can't continue to govern with one ski still on the doormat. Give me this job. I won't let you down.

Back to DIANA.

DIANA: So, what do you say?

ADAM: It'll create a lot of problems within the party. The ERG will accuse us of being the EU's political puppet. Maybe I made a mistake in offering you the post.

DIANA: Look, Adam, we've been in a state of diplomatic superposition for too long. We're struggling along, both simultaneously inside and outside the EU. You can't continue to govern over Schrodinger's Britain. Give me this job. I won't let you down.

Back to SIMON

SIMON: I see a flicker of conviction. Let me complete the task we started in twenty-sixteen.

ADAM: All right. You can have the job.

SIMON: Wonderful. But, how will you silence the Remainers in our ranks?

ADAM: That's my master-stroke. I'm giving the Brexit job to Diana Purdy.

SIMON: Then I rescind my decision. I have no interest in being a member of any government which includes that splenetic euro-lover.

ADAM: Unfortunately, I've already offered her the job and she's accepted.

SIMON: The grasping harridan.

ADAM: So, the only way to counter-balance her influence is for you to take up my offer.

SIMON: You want me to sit round the cabinet table – with Diana Purdy?

ADAM: Come on, Simon. Let's work together on moving Britain forward. Full steam ahead!

Back to DIANA.

DIANA: But… what will you say to the Brexiteers?

ADAM: That's my master-stroke. I'm giving the Trade job to Simon Cavendish.

DIANA: Simon!? I will not serve in the Cabinet if that pin-striped atrocity is given Trade.

ADAM: Unfortunately, I've already offered him the job and he's accepted.

DIANA: The little bastard.

ADAM: The only way to counter-balance his influence is for you to take up my offer.

DIANA: You want me to sit round the cabinet table – with Simon Cavendish?

ADAM: Come on, Diana. Let's work together on undoing this terrible mess. Full steam reverse!

Blackout.

SCENE SIX

The PM's office in Number 10. PAUL is sitting behind ADAM's desk. ADAM has a stack of newspapers and is reading out the headlines.

ADAM: "PM's full cabinet revealed. Adam Masters shows his class."

PAUL: I've seen it.

ADAM: "Shows his class". Do the Mail next.

PAUL: Adam, what is the point of this?

ADAM: I told you it would work! I told you. Do the Mail.

PAUL finds the Mail and reads the headline.

PAUL: "Simon Cavendish's appointment ends rumours that new PM Adam Masters has been seduced by the soft Brexiteers on the left of his party. This is a victory for the Tory right and for the country."

ADAM: "And for the country."

PAUL: But Adam…

ADAM: Now do The Guardian.

PAUL: "Simon Cavendish's elevation to cabinet level was unfortunate but it's in the inclusion of Diana Purdy that Masters demonstrates his true beliefs. The threat of hard Brexit is now over."

ADAM: Who says you can't please all of the people all of the time?

PAUL: Do you really imagine that the years of disagreements, factions, rows and punch-ups will all now cancel each other out in your miraculous peace and reconciliation re-shuffle?

ADAM: Even the bloody BBC sounded impressed. Do you know, John Humphrys managed to limit his condescension to just the hour before *Puzzles for Today.*

PAUL: Because first reports are drafts. Everyone thinks the budget sounds great for the first forty-eight hours until someone notices the tax plan introduces a surcharge on oxygen and the productivity plan merges Christmas with Easter.

ADAM: Moan, moan, moan... This is a fantastic start to my administration. And now that I've done everything in that file of yours...

PAUL: Which you haven't read. And no, you haven't.

ADAM: You need to keep your end of the bargain and join the team.

PAUL: There was no bargain.

ADAM: Are you <u>sure</u> there was no bargain?

PAUL: I think I'd remember.

ADAM: Look, some politicians are permanent outsiders. They revel in the luxury of free speech, but they never really have a chance to direct events. I've invited Diana and Simon to join me as insiders. Now they've seen real power, they will always be in our debt.

PAUL: Wonderful. A Faustian suicide pact. How could that possibly end badly?

ADAM: More like two major pieces permanently keeping each other in check.

PAUL: I don't think you realise just how long they've been waiting for something like this.

ADAM: What do you mean?

PAUL produces a fat bundle of papers.

PAUL: This is the policy paper, schedules and annexures prepared by your loyal new Brexit Secretary. This process essentially makes Britain a non-voting member of the European Union, with all the costs of membership, just none of the tedious representation.

He dumps the bundle on ADAM's desk.

ADAM: She's only been in the job twenty-four hours…

PAUL takes out a second, equally fat bundle…

PAUL: And this is the policy paper, supplements and codicils prepared by your devoted new Trade Secretary. This procedure essentially returns Britain to its post war glory days of untrammelled sovereignty, just without all that awful frictionless trade.

He dumps that bundle on ADAM's desk too.

ADAM: Right… well, we need to get officials to start going through all of this very carefully. Let's say that takes them three days per page. How many pages do you think are in each…?

PAUL: Do you seriously want to commit hundreds of civil service hours to studying these two mutually-contradictory courses of action?

ADAM: Officials love doing that sort of thing. Better than working on benefits, insurance and fishing rights.

PAUL: There are fourteen separate chapters on benefits, insurance and fishing rights in each dossier!

ADAM: How did they get it all done so fast?

PAUL: Both wings of the party supported you. So, both expected a share of the spoils. They've had their pet institutes and biased foundations working these up for months.

ADAM: I'm surprised they didn't give it another couple of weeks, for form's sake. Still, all it really does is accelerate the timetable a bit.

PAUL: Timetable? Wait, you knew this would happen?

ADAM: Maybe.

PAUL: And when were you going to tell me what you were planning?

ADAM: Not when your security pass is still half-in and half-out of the door of Number Ten!

PAUL: Well, sure. I mean if your administration stands for anything it's for not being half-in and half-out! I can't help you to deliver a strategy if I don't know what it is. So, start talking.

ADAM: Well, it's not a strategy as such. More an approach... a state of mind. That's what Brexit is really, isn't it? Not a thing but a process. A continuing series of emerging and adaptable policy positions which...

PAUL: *[A thought suddenly strikes him.]* Zugzwang!

ADAM: What?

PAUL: You're a chess-player. You know what zugzwang means.

ADAM: I've never heard that word before in my life.

PAUL: Then let me enlighten you. You're not in check now, but if you make any move at all, it can only weaken your position. Meaning that the best thing to do is to do nothing. Oh Jesus, that's your strategy, isn't it?

ADAM: Nonsense.

PAUL: But it's your turn to move.

ADAM: Eventually.

PAUL: So... you're just going to wait? For how long?

ADAM: When I played chess with my brother, and I got into this situation, sometimes if I waited long enough, he'd just have another go out of sheer boredom.

PAUL: This issue of Europe is a constant state of political zugzwang and your idea is to keep postponing the decisions for as long as possible, in the hope that something else will turn up!?

ADAM: Something always turns up.

PAUL: Something like what?!

ADAM: Something like anything! A ferocious outbreak of herpes in Dorset. A same-sex Royal wedding. The president nukes Arkansas for ratings. Any of those things could happen. We just need to keep praying for one of those things to happen.

PAUL: You <u>want</u> the transitional arrangements to keep going?

ADAM: Until something bigger or better comes along. We wait for something to change the rules of the game. But until then we continue with the policy of <u>frenetic inertia</u>, allowing each side to think they have something to show for their hard negotiating. The British are brilliant at pleasing both sides.

Some clauses in a treaty suit one side, some give a victory to the other. Balfour knew what he was doing with that declaration.

PAUL: Tell me you're not going to turn your attention to the Middle East.

ADAM: This is the will of people, Paul.

PAUL: A constant state of doubt and uncertainty?

ADAM: Exactly. The existence of that doubt and uncertainty is surely the only thing that people have left to hang on to. If we can't even be certain about that ambiguity, what can we be sure about ever again?

PAUL: So, you want me to join you in running a government that doesn't have any policies?

ADAM: What's the alternative? If this government falls, all we'll see is that bearded Labour Gandalf driving his motor-home up Downing Street, on the threshold of ushering in a new era of women-only bakeries and the nationalisation of shoes. Compared to that, having a government without any policies is a vital public service.

PAUL: At least he believes in something.

ADAM: Oh, come on, Paul!

PAUL: Sooner or later, Simon and Diana are going to want to hear from you. They'll want to see some progress on these proposals. You'll have to commit one way or the other.

ADAM: I'll talk to them in a few weeks. After the G7. Once the Lord Mayor's show is out of the way. When is Haley's comet due again?

PAUL: Your "strategy" is a temporary solution... like trying to hold back a hurricane with the power of positive thinking.

ADAM: Then take the job as chief of staff and help me find a better one.

PAUL: You come up with a policy that I can get behind and I'll think about it.

ADAM: Stalemate?

PAUL: Zugzwang.

Black out.

SCENE SEVEN

House of Commons corridor, some weeks later. PAUL is leaving the Prime Minister's office. SIMON glides up to him.

SIMON: Ah, Mr Connell, there you are.

PAUL: The PM's busy at the moment, Simon.

SIMON: Actually, it's you I wanted to talk to.

PAUL: Oh, good.

SIMON: I have to say, I've found the first few cabinet meetings rather trying. Especially being sat at the end where there is quite a strong draught. I can never seem to catch the PM's eye.

PAUL: I'm sorry to hear that…

SIMON: I understand that Diana has to be there. Appointing her as a sop to the Remainers, I can understand. But I cannot have a cabinet colleague trying to dismantle the engine of my legislative Daimler.

DIANA marches past, on her phone.

DIANA: *[Incandescent.]* No, I did not say the Home Secretary is obsessed with prisons… Yes, you can say he voted to intern his own teenagers but it's deep background. *[Beloved.]* Kiss kiss.

She hangs up and notices PAUL and SIMON.

DIANA: Well. What's the occasion for this intimate little gathering?

SIMON: I was just asking Mr Connell if he wanted a spare ticket for Covent Garden… Mrs Cavendish was coming but her dropsy has flared up again.

DIANA: It seems to me that important matters of state were being discussed in my absence.

SIMON: You need to realise that the PM gave me certain reassurances.

DIANA: Did he now?

SIMON: Yes, he did.

PAUL: Oh god…

PAUL does his best to melt into the background.

DIANA: Come on, Paul. The PM's had my dossier for weeks now. Is he taking my proposals seriously?

SIMON: I'm afraid that our magnificent leader may have been rather distracted from whatever insane stratagem you've presented him with. He's been going through my action plan with a very careful eye.

DIANA: What are you basing that on?

SIMON: Well, he's had the time to read it very thoroughly.

DIANA: So, when I hear nothing, I'm being ignored, but when you hear nothing, it's because he's being thorough? To you, confirmation bias is just a natural part of being alive isn't it?

SIMON: Ah, the doctrine of misguided treason. You refer to Thucydides, of course?

DIANA: Look, you may have a triple first in sycophancy and beef wellington but that doesn't give you the right...

PAUL groans and wades in, despite himself.

PAUL: Okay, both of you, shut up and listen to me. Why is that you Conservatives – who are usually so focused on winning power – always start losing your minds when it comes to Europe? You're doing everything you can to make sure that the EU destroys your own party.

SIMON: But don't you understand, Mr Connell? That's why the party has to destroy the EU!

DIANA: You see, he's insane!

SIMON: Am I? *[To PAUL.]* It strikes me that you are uniquely positioned to resolve this imbroglio. We politely seek guidance, as our leader appears to be hoisting two banners.

PAUL: He's the Prime Minister. And you're just going to have to trust him.

DIANA: I did trust him. But if he doesn't start making good on some of his promises to me, he shouldn't be too surprised if aspects of my action plan start appearing on Buzzfeed, Snapchat and Reddit.

SIMON: While I share my thoughts in a series of hard-hitting essays in Country Life.

PAUL chuckles quietly to himself.

PAUL: There's a motto displayed on the walls in some of the high offices of state in the various countries I've worked in. "Never start a media war with Paul Connell." Is that what you two are planning on?

A pause.

PAUL: I thought not.

SIMON: Except, you might pass on the singular word *[Patting his jacket pocket.]* "envelopes".

DIANA: For once, Simon has a point. I understand that we're up to forty.

SIMON: Not very far from lift off…

DIANA: And then… kaboom!

A pause.

PAUL: All right! I'll talk to him…

SCENE EIGHT

The Offices of the European Commission in Brussels.

HELENA: So, plans had to change. However, while deciding upon their next course of action, they decided to stay in the European Economic Area, purely as a brief interim measure.

ADAM: And when was that?

HELENA: Nineteen ninety-four. Still, you can't rush big decisions. Now, was there anything else you wanted to say?

ADAM: Yes actually.

HELENA: Go on then.

ADAM: Well, perhaps we could talk more technically?

He opens PAUL's file and clumsily fishes out a briefing paper.

ADAM: Is it possible we could consider whether the post-Maastricht convergence criteria could be retrospectively disapplied, so that the European Acquis doesn't necessarily have full force over mixed-use trade agreements…

HELENA moves over, snatches the paper and rips it up.

ADAM: This is just the sort of European intransigence that is standing between us and a meaningful long-term deal.

HELENA drops the pieces in the bin.

HELENA: You're accusing me of intransigence? You've just committed the biggest public policy fuck-up since appeasement.

ADAM: There really is no point in talking to you, is there?

HELENA: Not really. It was never us you were negotiating with in the first place. You really should have got your own house in order before you started the countdown.

ADAM: We had to trigger Article Fifty. The people had spoken!

HELENA: Exactly. You're not negotiating with us at all. And Article Fifty wasn't your backstop, it was-

ADAM: *[Interrupting.]* There is no need for that kind of language.

HELENA: Sorry, your *lifeline.* Article Fifty was designed to crush the position of any retreating nation. And you decided to trigger withdrawal almost immediately. A quick announcement that got you through one tricky day at a seaside conference.

ADAM: The EU at its devious best, eh, then?

HELENA: Article Fifty was drafted by the British.

ADAM: Right.

HELENA: If it's any consolation, I doubt anyone else could have done much better. Even if your Brexit failure will now very likely be the first line of your Wikipedia entry.

ADAM: But I wasn't to blame for globalisation. Or unemployment, or the cost of living or the financial crisis or immigration. It was a cascade of protest.

HELENA: The storming of the Bastille?

ADAM: I suppose I should be grateful that the guillotine is out of fashion.

HELENA: What will you do now?

ADAM: Perhaps try and improve my fading media profile by making documentaries about bird-watching and railway stations, while wearing pink and lemon corduroys.

HELENA: Do stop by and say hello.

ADAM: I doubt I'd be welcome here.

HELENA: You might be surprised. You're still a member of the club, don't forget.

ADAM: Which club?

HELENA: The leaders' club. And leaders always support ex-leaders because one day they will be one too.

ADAM: I'm not an ex-leader yet.

HELENA: No… but, as far as I can see, you do have only two alternatives. You give in to all of our demands, make the transition arrangements permanent and end up paying more and getting less. Or you boldly go it alone and watch your national economy wither. Either way, I don't see the British people celebrating your return from Brussels with a brass band and piccalilli.

ADAM: No. But there is another way. Possibly.

HELENA: What do you mean?

ADAM: We just… stop it.

HELENA: Stop what?

ADAM: Brexit. We just stop it. Reverse it. Pretend it never happened.

HELENA: Pretend?

ADAM: Oh, you know what I mean. If I get crucified for delivering a soft Brexit and the economy gets slaughtered in a hard Brexit – what price would I have to pay for no Brexit at all?

HELENA stares at him in wonderment.

SCENE NINE

Back in the Prime Minister's study in the House of Commons. PAUL has a stack of newspapers in front of him. He seems uncharacteristically cheerful.

PAUL: Want me to read them out?

ADAM: No, I don't!

PAUL: *[Ignoring him.]* Why don't we start with The Mail? "Simon Cavendish side-lined. The pro-Brexit trade secretary is out of favour. Was his appointment nothing more than an artless piece of political theatre from a Prime Minister who has already lost control of his cabinet?"

ADAM: I've read it. Thank you.

PAUL: I wonder who leaked that? Did you see The Times?

ADAM: Yes!!

PAUL: *[Heedless.]* "Our dithering PM has become a leader who would prefer to contrive than decide." And an unnamed Cabinet Minister describes you as "starving to death between two bales of hay, the political manifestation of Buridan's ass".

ADAM: I know. I know. What are you going to do about it?!

PAUL: Oh, it'll blow over. Isn't that the whole keystone of your "zugzwang" strategy?

ADAM: This is different. I can't go another day with headlines like this.

PAUL: If you want to look at it this way, it's a triumph. The two most ideologically-opposed politicians in the entire country are finally united – in their hatred and distrust of you. Apparently if you stay in zugzwang long enough, the black and white pieces start working together of their own accord.

ADAM: That is not a legal move.

PAUL: I'm serious, Adam. They're threatening envelopes. The Chairman now has forty letters from your baleful MPs calling for a leadership vote. If their supporters post him just a handful more…

ADAM: Ah, well, you may find that the Chairman is getting rather forgetful in his old age. Oh, butter-fingers, there goes another envelope down the back of the tea-room sofa. Where exactly did I put that pearl-handled letter-opener?

PAUL: You've bought him off!?

ADAM: That's an outrageous suggestion! It is amazing though what the offer of a knighthood can do for a geriatric legislator from the county set. Anyway, it's a PM's lot in life to have virtually the entire cabinet out to get you. That's why keeping them at each other's throats is such an advantage. It's the bloody press I'm worried about.

PAUL: Okay, I do have one idea for you. It'll give the great headlines you can't get enough of, and it will stop Simon and Diana from joining forces against you.

ADAM: Brilliant! What do I have to do?

PAUL: Pick one of their proposals and publicly back it. At a stroke you castrate one and elevate the other, severing their partnership forever. And at the same time, the press will be full of stories about your decisive leadership.

ADAM: I can't betray their trust like that! What about my united and principled government?

PAUL: Rapidly becoming a decaying and war-torn government.

ADAM: It's too soon. I can't deploy the end game yet. How many days left to Bonar Law?

PAUL: A hundred and sixty-three. But, Adam, you can't let that govern your decision-making.

ADAM: Can't I? I've thought of little else since <u>you</u> brought it up. It haunts my nights and infects my days.

PAUL: Then you need to move forward.

ADAM: All right then. Hypothetically. If I did decide to put one of these proposals into action – which one should it be?

PAUL: Oh, no… I win campaigns. Policies I leave to politicians.

ADAM: How convenient. I'm only asking for an opinion. You're usually overflowing with those.

PAUL: *[Tense.]* This decision will dictate the entire future of the United Kingdom.

ADAM: Then let's hear your point of view! Come on, Paul! During the leadership contest, you never held back from telling me what speech to make, which tie to wear, or which constituency to visit. Why is it when…

PAUL: *[Interrupting.]* Pick Simon's.

ADAM: What?

PAUL: Diana's plan is a hugely-detailed exercise in doing nothing at all. Eighteen months of even more white papers, reorganisations and consultations that will leave us in the same situation we're in now. It won't work. It will look like a fudge. Implement Simon's plan and you're a visionary.

ADAM: Can't we stage some kind of media stunt instead? What are the Red Arrows doing tomorrow?

PAUL: Good prime ministers are fighters. But the best are gamblers.

ADAM: Bets can be lost! Like launching a war and – oh, whoopsie – finding there were no chemical weapons after all. Holding and losing a referendum. Calling a general election campaign that slowly converts you from Joan of Arc to Jimmy Krankie. If I have to, and I mean have to, pick one of these proposals, then Diana's at least stands a chance of getting through the Commons, even if it does achieve buggery fuck-all.

PAUL: Then, that's it. I'm at the end. You keep telling me I have to stay. But every single time I offer advice, I'm rebuffed, fobbed off, criticised, contradicted or shouted down. And you wonder why I don't want to be here?

ADAM: I thought we were friends.

PAUL: So did I.

ADAM: But I'm doing what you wanted. I'm backing one of these proposals!

PAUL: You're backing the wrong one!!

ADAM: Oh...

ADAM sits, stunned at the realisation.

ADAM: I see, I see now... of course...

PAUL: What's going on?

ADAM turns to look at him.

ADAM: You voted Leave.

PAUL: What do you mean?

ADAM: You're a closet Brexiteer.

PAUL: This is not about me. This is about your long-term survival.

ADAM: I don't think it is. Attempting to get a full on hard Brexit through the House is the one thing that might unite the Labour Mods and Rockers long enough for them to remember they're meant to be opposing the government.

PAUL: Possibly.

ADAM: So why would you advise me to back that bill? Can it be that I've finally uncovered a seam of principle beneath that ideological permafrost?

PAUL: Simon has the numbers. Read his proposal. We can do it.

ADAM: We? You are taking the job, then?

PAUL: No.

ADAM: I see. So, you're happy for me to try and launch this missile at our EU colleagues, but you want to give yourself plenty of time to head for the bunker before the inevitable blowback.

PAUL: That's what an advisor is!! The buck doesn't stop with me, it stops with you. If you're so worried about what the press are saying about you, stop writing their headlines for them and be a prime minister. This time I mean it. I'm leaving and I'm not coming back.

ADAM: I don't accept your resignation.

PAUL: You don't have to accept my resignation because I never took the job.

ADAM: Then you can't resign. If you never took the job, then you can't resign from it.

PAUL: Adam, I'm not playing Brexit Through The Looking Glass with you. Listen, and try and understand. I don't want to be your chief of staff because I don't trust you anymore. I'm going home.

ADAM: Paul…

PAUL: Never call me again.

PAUL leaves.

ADAM sighs. He picks up the phone.

ADAM: Diana Purdy please. Oh, hello, Diana. I wonder if you could…

DIANA Purdy enters, phone to her ear.

DIANA: Yes, I'm on my way. Just need to finish the other call… *[Ballistic.]* No I'm not saying the Pensions Secretary is dour, I've just met more happy-go-lucky coroners. *[Gushing.]* Love you lots. *[She hangs up.]* Hello Adam.

ADAM: Diana… How wonderful to see you! Have you been waiting outside long?

DIANA: I have got the office just next door.

ADAM: That's the Foreign Secretary's office.

DIANA: That rather explains all the looks.

ADAM: And how are things going at Brexit HQ itself and its no doubt crack team of officials?

DIANA: Oh wonderful. I turned up on day one to discover that they've made no proper plans to leave the EU even after we've left the EU and their first agenda item was to ask me about my policy on secondments, transfers and early retirements.

ADAM: Right…

DIANA: Which is why I need to press you on some decisions. You gave me a very clear undertaking…

ADAM: …that I would pay Simon lip-service until we were ready to implement your proposals. And we now are. Your bill making the terms of the transition deal permanent is now official Government policy.

DIANA: Really?!

ADAM: Yes… if you think we can get it through the House?

DIANA: I know we can. The Transition Tories can do a deal with the Hard-Blue Labour-Remainers and the Soft-Hard Tory Re-Joiners. With the rest of the cabinet on our side, that gets us over the line with a few votes to spare.

ADAM: Marvellous.

DIANA: You know, there was some whispering that the only thing you were interested in was your own political survival!

ADAM: Ridiculous. And I'm glad you're the first to know my decision. Simon's proposals... well...

He picks up SIMON's proposals and throws them in the bin.

ADAM: Turgid and unworkable.

DIANA: Better not let Simon hear you say that, eh?

ADAM: Yes, about that. I think it's important that Simon gets to hear this direct from me. We must get away from leaking and public innuendo. I need to tell him directly. You know how much I hate party conflict.

There are some taps on the door.

SIMON: *[From outside.]* Prime Minister? Might I have a word?

ADAM: *[Panicked.]* Simon...

DIANA: What's the matter?

SIMON: *[From outside.]* It's me. Simon.

ADAM: Simon... it's Simon!

DIANA: Shall I show him in?

ADAM: No, no, no...

DIANA: I'll show him in. *[Louder, to SIMON.]* Come in, come in, Simon. I'm here with Adam. We're here waiting for you!

She opens the door and SIMON floats in.

SIMON: Prime Minister... Diana. How delightful to see you both.

ADAM: Have you also been waiting outside?

SIMON: Well the Commons is quite small really. All the better to see the more interesting comings and goings.

ADAM: Actually, I'm a bit busy at the moment. Could we reschedule? They've just found knotweed in Big Ben... the Isle of Wight is threatening independence... You haven't got the latest timings for Haley's Comet have you?

DIANA: Adam's just joking.

SIMON: Well then Prime Minister, now I don't have to attract your attention via Cabinet loud-hailer, why don't you declaim your proclamation forthwith?

ADAM: What...?

DIANA: Adam has come to a decision. Haven't you, Adam?

ADAM: Yes.

SIMON: That's wonderful to hear.

DIANA: And he wants to tell you personally. Face to face. Don't you, Adam?

ADAM: Hmmm, yes, hmmmm...

A pause.

DIANA stares at ADAM.

DIANA: Shall I tell him them?

ADAM: No, Diana!

ADAM looks from one of the them to the other, looking increasingly desperate.

SIMON: Tell me what?!

DIANA: *[Furious.]* Are you reneging on our deal? You want to renege on a deal thirty seconds after you've done it?!

SIMON: What deal? You've done a deal?!

ADAM: There is no deal. Well, there is a deal... just not the deal, you think, we thought that, a different deal... oh god...

Suddenly, SIMON notices something.

SIMON: What's that?

ADAM: What's what?

SIMON: In the bin.

ADAM: What bin?

They both stare at the bin.

SIMON: It's my proposal!

ADAM: No, it isn't.

He fishes it out.

SIMON: It bloody well is.

ADAM: Oh that!

SIMON: Yes, that.

ADAM: How did that get there?

DIANA: You just threw it in there!

ADAM: No!

DIANA: You said it was turgid and unworkable!

SIMON: You said what?!

DIANA: You said that we're going to make the transition arrangements permanent. That it's now official government policy.

SIMON is stung.

SIMON: This country's ability to have an independent trade policy is an absolute red line.

ADAM: Must it be a red line? Couldn't we make it a pink line?

SIMON: For the past forty years we've been seeking competitive advantage within the European Union. Now we can seek those advantages across the entire world.

DIANA: Yes, of course. The UK can break loose from its own moorings to snuffle out new trading opportunities across the known galaxy. This is the first time in human history that anyone has tried to negotiate a trade deal that's worse than the one they are already in. We might as well declare sanctions on ourselves!

ADAM: A pinkish line? An off-white line with an occasional hint of pink?

DIANA: Unless this swashbuckling new approach to free trade means flogging off the production of passports and warm beer to Holland, in which case – welcome back, protectionism and hard borders.

SIMON: You'll never get this through the House. With the opposition of the Tory Hard-Liners, the Soft Red Labour Leavers and the continuity DUP, there will be a clear blocking majority. I won't be your obedient little help-meet.

DIANA: Oh, why don't you write it up for the Times? A ten-page Sunday supplement detailing your latest oil slick of opinion.

ADAM: Maybe we could just find a good old Tory compromise?

SIMON: On the issue of Europe there can be no compromise.

DIANA: And there it is. This isn't politics any more, it's theology! Let's consult the foundational texts and bow down before the Great Ark of the Euro-Sceptic Covenant. "Praise be, praise be to the vast majesty that is Brexit!"

SIMON: Was that a hidden reference to Plutarch you smuggled in there?

DIANA: No, it wasn't!

SIMON: Diana. Look, I know why you're upset. It's because you were used to winning. Everyone on the remain side was always so used to winning. The banks, industry, broadcasting, big business, the mainstream of the Tory and Labour parties. For once the establishment lost and it's made you all absolutely seething.

A pause.

DIANA: Why don't you just fuck off?

SIMON: Right, well... I'm glad that you have at least made a decision, Prime Minister. But I think it's time for me to leave with my honour intact.

He glides out.

ADAM: Right. What... did he actually mean by that?

DIANA: I think he's just resigned.

ADAM: Has he? How can we find out?!

DIANA: Check Twitter!

ADAM: I haven't got a phone.

DIANA: You haven't got a phone?!

ADAM: They took it away from me when I entered Downing Street. Along with my passport.

DIANA: You're the most powerful man in Britain and you're not allowed to have a passport or a phone?

ADAM: And after that they show you the Cabinet Room where you're invited to make decisions while presiding over a table that's shaped like a coffin.

DIANA: Wait, I'll check mine...

DIANA fishes out her phone and begins stabbing inexpertly at the screen.

DIANA: I'm linked into the Tory MP's WhatsApp group. Let me have a look. Nothing yet... just the usual self-congratulatory messages, fake praise and enquiries about the cheapest dry cleaners on the Horseferry Road... Hang on, I've got it...

ADAM and DIANA crowd round the phone.

DIANA: He says... Simon yes... he's... he's just Tweeted... "I have today resigned from the Cabinet and will be making a personal statement to the House of Commons this afternoon. Hashtag tick-tock, tick-tock." What does that mean?

ADAM: Look out for ticking time-bombs.

DIANA: Should I reply?! Oh shit... I've just liked his Tweet.

ADAM: Unlike it! They'll say it's a plot... a conspiracy to undermine the PM.

DIANA: I'm not sure how... how do I unlike it?! Do I press... oh, oh... I think that's now a re-tweet... yes, yes, I've now re-tweeted it...

ADAM snatches the phone, stabs at it, throws it into a bin and glares at DIANA.

DIANA: I'm sure there's no need to look like that.

ADAM: Diana, we have about three minutes before this entire administration collapses under the weight of its own contradictions! What the hell are we going to do!? The press are going to crucify me. We should issue a D-Notice. Order a blanket ban. Execute every third Dimbleby.

DIANA: No!

ADAM: Okay, okay, let's spread a rumour that Simon's had a breakdown. He's an alcoholic. A depressed alcoholic. A manic-depressive, pathological alcoholic with an Oedipus complex and a sinister aversion to oboes.

DIANA: I thought you hated party conflict?

ADAM: Of course I fucking do!!

DIANA: Adam! Snap out of it. We can survive this. We need a media plan.

ADAM: A media plan? Yes! Yes, that's what we need! A plan! A media plan!

DIANA: We need to show them we are taking firm and decisive action in Simon's absence. We need a compelling narrative.

ADAM: Narrative… narrative…

DIANA: Yes Adam, what's your narrative?

ADAM: I'm in a complete fucking panic and I don't know what to do?!

DIANA: We need to make a proper statement.

ADAM: Um, okay, okay… say I've agreed to back your version of Brexit. That is now the official position of Her Majesty's Government.

DIANA: We're making the transition arrangements permanent. We will be staying in a permanent Customs Union…

ADAM: Therefore, we can't secure extra trade deals anyway. So…

DIANA: So… we don't need a Trade Secretary. We can spin it that it was all part of the plan.

ADAM: Yes! We'll say I always intended to merge the Trade and Brexit departments together!

DIANA: When you decided to make the transition arrangements permanent, it became clear Simon was redundant.

ADAM: His resignation is therefore merely an ongoing statement of Government policy.

DIANA: That's brilliant.

ADAM: I have my moments.

DIANA: There's no way Simon can survive this. Never start a media war with Paul Connell.

ADAM stares at her – his panic returning. Then…

ADAM: Very well put.

Blackout.

SCENE TEN

Brussels.

HELENA: No Brexit at all? A fascinating proposal.

ADAM: Would the EU agree?

HELENA: I don't know. I mean, at this stage it would be tantamount to treating you as a new applicant. You'd be in the queue behind Albania and Kosovo. And I'm not sure how well your economy is doing in comparison.

ADAM: We can compete. Free trade, encouraging investment…

HELENA: Massive de-regulation and slashing corporate taxes.

ADAM: Something like that.

HELENA: Making Britain great again as some sort of gigantic version of Guernsey?

ADAM: We all need to compromise.

HELENA: Well, we probably would let you back in. And for an upfront payment we might be able to move you up the queue a bit. But there are a few extra conditions.

ADAM: Such as?

HELENA: You would lose the rebate of course. Pay more than you ever did before.

ADAM: We have put you through a lot of unnecessary difficulty and angst. We'd probably accept that. Anything else?

HELENA: You'd lose the veto.

ADAM: At least we'd have a seat at the table again.

HELENA: And, I think we would insist that you promised not to have another Brexit vote for the foreseeable future. We don't want to go through that again.

ADAM: I could make that promise. But it wouldn't technically be binding.

HELENA: You said that about the referendum.

ADAM: Yes, yes... All right... All right... is that finally it?

HELENA: Just one more thing. And I'm afraid it might be a bit of a deal-breaker.

ADAM: I'll consider anything at this point.

HELENA: Anything?

ADAM: Yes, for God's sake. I have to have an alternative.

HELENA: At this stage, I would have thought no deal would be an easier sell. The Remainers can't trust you any more, surely?

ADAM: The Brexiteers think I'm a traitor. The Remainers only think I'm incompetent. You can manage incompetence. My only real option now is re-joining.

HELENA: I wouldn't be so sure of that.

ADAM: Helena – what are the extra conditions for re-entry?

HELENA: One final thing.

ADAM: Yes?

HELENA: Just a little thing, really.

ADAM: Which would be?

HELENA: Monetary union. I think we would insist this time that you join the Euro…

A pause.

HELENA: …and abolish the pound.

ADAM gasps in horror.

Black out.

SCENE ELEVEN

PAUL is at home, working on his laptop, on a mobile phone. There is an arm-chair. He is in mid-conversation.

PAUL: Well, think of me as a disinterested third party… okay… Bye, Alex. *[He hangs up.]*

The doorbell rings. PAUL gets up and lets SIMON in.

PAUL: Come on in. Can I get you anything? Tea? Coffee? *[He tries a better guess.]* Sherry…?

SIMON: I'm afraid I've gone teetotal. Mrs Cavendish insists that I'm poised for the battles to come.

PAUL: Of course she does.

SIMON: So, Paul Connell, the man who could get Caligula elected on a family values ticket, turns out to have some political convictions of his own.

PAUL: The people generally get to the right decision.

SIMON: Which is why we have to stop this disastrous bill.

PAUL: Then you need the votes. But you don't have the Irish.

SIMON: One of the drawbacks of trying to negotiate this kind of affair from the lowly position of the backbenches. I was sizing up some potential rebels, but they were disappointingly grateful for another half billion from our brand-new Treasury-approved 3D money printer.

PAUL: What has Adam promised them?

SIMON: Most of them were bought off with offers of new infrastructure for their constituencies. Three hospitals, two schools and in one case a vineyard. Another four are now looking forward to their retirements as high-level envoys to a number of Caribbean islands. I was quite tempted myself.

PAUL: And that makes it tight. And bear in mind, defeating this bill is one thing. Ending the transitional arrangements are another.

SIMON: Once we've defeated Diana's bill, Adam's personal authority will be in tatters. Then I'll redouble my efforts. I've met with seventeen MPs in the past four days alone. More private tête-à-têtes. More solo audiences. I will win that argument, one intimate conversation at a time.

PAUL: Please don't do that Simon.

SIMON: What do you mean?

PAUL: I've been tracking the data for the past two weeks. The number of undecideds, the people we can actually influence, is small. Maybe no more than thirty.

SIMON: That's why I've been working so hard to meet them all personally.

PAUL: And almost without exception, everyone you've met personally has later told me that they're going to vote with the government.

SIMON: What?

PAUL: Everyone you have a private tête-à-tête with, subsequently decides that they want to see your tête on a spike. The one thing your mission really doesn't need, is you. For some reason, your brand of smug, supercilious condescension just isn't landing with your fellow MPs.

SIMON: You want me resign from my own campaign?!

PAUL: It might actually increase your popularity.

SIMON: How flattering.

PAUL: I just need you to leave this to me. Adam has almost no chance of getting this bill through, and that means he has almost no chance of survival. Unless you screw it up. So don't call anyone. Don't talk to anyone. Don't do anything. Just show up on Wednesday night and quietly walk through the no lobby. Got it?

SIMON: Thank you, Paul, for your brutal and refreshing honesty.

PAUL: You're welcome. Now, fuck off out of my house.

Black out.

SCENE TWELVE

ADAM is in his Commons office. SIMON is standing at stage right. ADAM is pacing, centre-stage. SIMON stares at him.

ADAM: Please. Call off this pointless rebellion.

SIMON: I'm afraid it's gone a bit too far for that.

ADAM: If you can't do this for me, then do it for the Cabinet. For the party. For the country.

SIMON: I am doing this for the country. Who are you doing it for?

The lighting changes revealing DIANA standing at stage left and plunging SIMON's side of the stage into darkness.

ADAM: Diana, please. We have to stop Simon's insurrection.

DIANA: I'm afraid it's gone a bit too far for that. He has enough rebels on side now to win his wrecking amendment. We're finished if he does. I'll have to resign.

ADAM: No, no, no…

DIANA: What else could I do? It would be a humiliation.

Back to SIMON.

ADAM: Call it off, Simon. I can make it worth your while. I'll put you back into Cabinet.

SIMON: There isn't a vacancy.

ADAM: Maybe you could be the next Brexit Secretary. You'd have carte blanche to introduce whatever policy you want.

SIMON: Once the delicate flower of trust has been trampled, it can never be coaxed back into bloom.

Back to DIANA.

ADAM: Please don't resign. You have to stay. We've been together in this thing from the start.

DIANA: You only appointed me to counter-balance Simon. What have you offered him to call off the rebellion?

ADAM: What makes you think I've offered him anything?

DIANA: I'm starting to understand the way you think. Did you offer him my job?

ADAM: Diana!! How could you!?

DIANA: Did he turn you down?

Back to SIMON.

SIMON: Sorry, Adam, I just don't think there's anything else you can offer me.

ADAM: Yes, yes there is! You could become the next Lord Privy Seal... I'll throw in three extra Seals! A luxury CBE? An audience with the Queen. A daily audience with the Queen.

SIMON: I see enough of her as it is. She is Mrs Cavendish's second cousin, after all

Back to DIANA.

ADAM: Any other job you want. I'll move Gavin to Justice and make him Lord Chancellor – he'll love that – he's got an O Level in Law. That opens up the Home Office for you... think what that did for Matron!

DIANA: I don't think so.

ADAM: We have to get through this.

DIANA: You're going to lose. And perhaps that's only fair because I know that you never really believed in what we were trying to do anyway.

ADAM: What… do you mean?

DIANA: I had to look zugzwang up… but it was very illuminating when I did. Paul took me through the approach carefully. He was a real asset to the administration, wasn't he? You were careless to let him go.

Back to SIMON.

SIMON: And, of course, I'm enormously grateful to Paul. Without his help, it's possible that this plucky rebellion would have struggled to lift-off.

ADAM: A real asset to my administration.

SIMON: For as long as your administration lasts, anyway.

ADAM: What?

SIMON repairs to his pocket and retrieves an envelope.

SIMON: My letter to the Chairman of the Ninety Twenty-Two. I believe this will be number forty-seven in his treacherous collection.

Back to DIANA.

DIANA: But now Paul has left you, it really is all over.

ADAM: What?!

She produces an envelope.

DIANA: My letter to the Chairman. I think this will now make it forty-eight. Election time.

ADAM: You and Simon. You've been in this together from the start, haven't you?

DIANA: Oh, Prime Minister you're becoming paranoid. Still, who would have thought that the two extremes…

Back to SIMON.

SIMON: …might combine against the middle. *[He looks at his watch.]* Time to vote soon.

The Division Bell rings thunderously.

SIMON: The very best of British, prime minister.

He leaves. ADAM is left forlornly on the stage.

SCENE THIRTEEN

PAUL's flat. The television is on, and news of the Commons defeat can be softly heard. Pundits are weighing-up ADAM's chances of holding on. The doorbell rings and he goes to answer it. He returns.

PAUL: I told you never to call me again.

ADAM follows him in, looking grim.

ADAM: I never was very good at listening to your advice.

PAUL: Well, you didn't even get close to Bonar Law's record. But maybe if you can cling onto until just past the Lord Mayor's show. Then you will officially be the ninety days Prime Minister. Great title for the memoirs.

PAUL turns off the TV with a remote control.

ADAM: I notice Simon backed off just days before the vote. I was rather counting on his smug, supercilious condescension to put off some potential rebels.

PAUL: Campaign managers need to tell politicians the hard truths. The good ones listen.

ADAM: Since then I've had thirty-five missed calls from the Chairman of the Nineteen Twenty-Two. He's going to trigger a new leadership election. God save us all if Derek Gadd's now our future. I hope you're pleased with yourself.

PAUL: It was the will of the people, Adam. Look, I've spent years winning and losing votes and winning and losing elections. And I would do anything to win. But once the result is delivered, it needs to be respected.

ADAM: That's a good sound bite but I don't think it's the real reason.

PAUL: It is.

ADAM: I know you, Paul.

PAUL: Brexit is the most complex public policy challenge since the Second World War… and they sent you to deal with it?! They sent you?!

ADAM: I needed you. And you abandoned me. No – you turned on me! You turned on me and for what… for ideology! You betrayed our friendship for ideology.

PAUL: I don't think it was me who betrayed our friendship.

ADAM: What are you talking about?

PAUL: I couldn't understand why you were so eager to have me as your chief of staff. Then I started to put it together. Most Prime Ministers surround themselves with a host of advisors. There are two benefits to that. If you don't like what one has to say, you can wander down the corridor and get a more reassuring diagnosis…

ADAM: Paul…

PAUL: *[Snapping at him.]* I haven't finished. Second, you don't get too associated with any one person. You don't become a double act. If you need to fire them, you can do it quietly and without fuss.

ADAM: I would probably have rounded out the team a bit more fully in due course…

PAUL: But you wanted me standing next to you when you won the contest. You wanted to share the glory with me. And after that, you hounded me every day. You wanted a sidekick. You wanted the world to know your best friend Paul Connell was standing with you, shoulder-to-shoulder. Your ultra-capable political Svengali.

ADAM: That's not what happened…

PAUL: I was your endgame, wasn't I? Delay, delay, delay. Whack the issue down the road. Pivot on every distraction. Ignite a different story. Sorry, folks, an actual decision has had to be put off again – and again – and again. But what if you run out of distractions? Be great to have something in your back pocket wouldn't it? Can't fire a cabinet minister. That runs the risk of dividing the party. And there's no point firing an advisor nobody has ever heard of, so… make me your way to break out of zugzwang.

ADAM: Paul…

PAUL: *[Pressing on.]* You beg and plead and cajole and blackmail me into running your campaign for you. Just so when the moment is right, when you're entirely out of options, when the strategy has self-destructed, then you can fire the hugely prominent chief-of-staff who gave you this terrible Brexit strategy and redeem yourself with the public and the party. Very clever. Brilliant even.

ADAM: I have my moments.

PAUL: Just a shame about the poor bastard you throw to the jackals!

A pause.

ADAM: A true friend would have welcomed the opportunity to serve in this way.

PAUL: What!?

ADAM: I would have taken care of you. After a suitable interlude. A peerage… or an introduction to some new campaign work abroad.

PAUL: I can find my own campaign work.

ADAM: *[Ignoring this.]* I was actually hoping you'd come with me to Brussels.

PAUL: Brussels?

ADAM: I'm meeting Helena Brandt first thing tomorrow. I've got no credible excuse to put her off any longer.

PAUL: You've been Prime Minister for three months and you've never met the Chief EU negotiator?

ADAM: We exchanged emails. Some incredibly cordial phone calls.

PAUL: It was in the file, Adam. Get the EU negotiator on your side as soon as possible. How many times have you cancelled on her?

ADAM: Three or four…

PAUL: It's like trying to bargain with a lemming.

ADAM: No, no… don't you see? This might still be survivable. If I come back from this meeting with a really imaginative proposal, I might still be able to get them back on-side. But I need you there with me. I need you, Paul.

PAUL: You're on your own.

Lights fade.

SCENE FOURTEEN

Brussels.

HELENA: Monetary union. I think we would insist this time that you join the Euro…

A pause.

HELENA: …and abolish the pound.

ADAM gasps in horror.

HELENA: Would that require a referendum?

ADAM slumps in a chair, broken, defeated.

ADAM: It's over. I've got nothing to go back to, except a House of Commons in flames, a cabinet in disarray, a right-wing press that despises me for my every action – even though I tried my hardest not to take any. And a left-wing press that despises me for my beliefs – even though I tried my hardest not to have any!

HELENA: Yes. Still, from our point of view, this has been quite satisfactory. While the transitional arrangements are still in place, we will continue trading with each other, you'll keep paying us money, but we won't have you there to veto budgets or generally make a nuisance of yourselves. I think it's called taking back control.

ADAM: Brexit doesn't mean Brexit?

HELENA: Finally, he understands! And now, thanks to your noble self-sacrifice, it will be ten years at least before anyone tries to alter the transition arrangement in any way at all.

ADAM: Even to make it permanent? I mean, that's the same as leaving it as it is, surely?

HELENA: No, no, no. If you actually want the transition deal to be made permanent, the last thing you should do is actually write that down in law.

ADAM: Really?

HELENA: If you go around telling people that it's going to be like this forever, you raise all sorts of unwanted questions in their minds. Do I actually want this? Is this what I signed up for? Just how long is forever anyway? Forty percent of marriages end in divorce, but do you know how many unmarried couples get divorced? Zero percent.

She strokes his upper arm and looks at him fondly.

ADAM: That doesn't make sense.

HELENA: Of course not. To you.

ADAM: What do you mean?

HELENA: Adam, when it comes to the EU, all British prime ministers have essentially been outsiders. Lacking power and influence. Have you ever thought what it might be like being an insider rather than an outsider?

ADAM: Go on.

HELENA: As I say, the Commission is very grateful for your efforts to protect the European project – at some cost to yourself.

She repairs to the drinks cabinet and pours ADAM a large glass of red wine.

ADAM: What do you mean… grateful?

HELENA: At home, you may be seen as a weak prime minister who craved approval more than the long-term interests of the world, his nation, or even his party. But many people here see you as a true European. A man who understands that it's in the best interests of the entire continent for Britain to be forced to continue to provide us with financial support. And even better if Britain ceases to have any input into how we spend it.

ADAM takes the wine.

ADAM: You know, I've only ever had the best interests of the EU at heart.

HELENA: I always said so. Now, we will shortly need to appoint a new High Representative for Climate Change. Based here in Brussels of course, but with a world-wide portfolio. And a suitably agreeable salary…

ADAM: I see. High Representative for Climate Change?

HELENA: I'd hate to see your talents go to waste.

ADAM: Well, climate change is the kind of problem which requires careful consideration and will not be helped by a rush to hasty action.

HELENA: You're going to do wonderfully well here, I can see.

They clink glasses.

HELENA: Welcome to the European Union.

Curtain.

Beethoven's Ninth Symphony, Movement Four.

The Ode to Joy.